OBLIGATORY COVID CHAPBOOK

OBLIGATORY COVID CHAPBOOK

March to Year-End 2020

STEPHEN M. HONIG

OBLIGATORY COVID CHAPBOOK: March to Year-End 2020

Published by Gatekeeper Press

2167 Stringtown Rd, Suite 109

Columbus, OH 43123-2989

www.GatekeeperPress.com

Copyright © 2021 by Stephen M. Honig

All rights reserved. Neither this book, nor any parts within it may be sold or reproduced in any form or by any electronic or mechanical means, including information storage and retrieval systems without permission in writing from the author. The only exception is by a reviewer, who may quote short excerpts in a review.

The cover design, interior formatting, typesetting, and editorial work for this book are entirely the product of the author. Gatekeeper Press did not participate in and is not responsible for any aspect of these elements.

ISBN (paperback): 9781662908033

Contents

Author's Statement:	11
Holding Hands	13
School Assignment/Take Home Quiz (of course)	15
Party—March, 2020	16
March, 2020	17
No News is Good News	19
My Sequential Recordation of My Thoughts Upon Arising Today, April 10, 2020 at 8:14 AM In Newton Massachusetts	20
Love in the Age of Spring	22
Moment of Fame	23
Me and Katya in the Forest	26
Notebook Entries/June 2020	28
Fear (summer of 2020)	31
August 1, 2020	33
Suburban Halloween Party	36
Thanksgiving Tent	39
Holiday Poem	41
Colored Lights	43
Disorder	46
Real Reel	49
A Walk On the Wild Side	51
About the Sky in Time of Pandemic	52
Dead Men Walking....	53
Gray	54
It's the End	56

*There is no single dedication of this work.
It belongs to all who have lived during the
year 2020; those who survived the year, and
particularly those who have not.*

"Many continued hoping that the epidemic
would soon die out and they and their families
be spared. Thus they felt under no obligation to
make any change in their habits, as yet.
Plague was an unwelcome visitant,
bound to take its leave one day
as unexpectedly as it had come."
– Albert Camus, The Plague

"Who WAS that masked man?"
—Attributed to numerous townspeople
in the Old West.

Author's Statement:

This volume is obligatory in the sense that I was compelled to write it. Everyone alive to read this book has a deep personal history at least equal to that contained in the poems below. That history may be on paper, on film, or in the most subtle and tangled of media: memory.

My hope is that the aggregate of the literature and images from the last ten months of the year 2020 will serve as a textured record of events which, for many, are and will remain the most insane and unsettling experiences of their lives. The human record often consists of official histories, governmental records, writings with a point to prove or a lesson to be derived. Poetry is a medium that strips away all but felt thought that we sometimes call emotion. Poems are the internal history of life.

Holding Hands

I am holding your hand.
You may not feel it, see it, even know it, but
your hand and mine
are entwined.

I am holding his hand.
He may not feel it, see it, even know it, but
his hand and mine
are entwined.

I am holding her hand.
She may not feel it, see it, even know it, but
her hand and mine
are entwined.

I am holding all their hands.
They surely do not all feel it, see it, even know it, but
their hands and mine
Are entwined.

We are in this together
although we do not understand the "this."
We know we all must pull together
if we are going to survive all of this.
We know that tomorrow can be better
if we all go together through this.
So forward then, as we hold each others' hands.

All well and good, I said to myself
and then things began to go South.
I tingled my fingers
in search of you, of him, or her, of them--
*

*

for a while
*

*

long time it seemed, and
I did not feel it, see it,
 began to doubt it
 when
*

*

I again felt fingers, pulled at palms, dug nails into flesh
and was renewed.
Tears dropped onto my cheeks
and I shook with promise,
reached up to wipe my tears, because
I, you, he, her, they were all saved, all entwined.

Then, I looked down, and
I was holding only my own clasped hands.

School Assignment/Take Home Quiz (of course)

Economy crashes.
Savings wiped out.
People die.
Poor people and old people and sick people particularly vulnerable.
It is raining and dark in Boston.
Children are petrified.
Toilet paper is scarce.
What is the date?
It is Friday the 13th.
Assignment: write a poem using above as outline.
Due: 3-13-20.
Question: is outline already a poem?
Grade: A+, if "yes" is your answer.

Party—March, 2020

They fiddled with their devices
and laughed at slightest provocation.

They moved from side to side
to center themselves on the screen.

They spoke in artificial cadence
when called upon to extend birthday wishes.

They held up glasses to be seen,
opaque with liquids of different colors.

They felt fulfilled with the fervor of the herd
and smiled until the lights went out.

They returned to their aloneness
And their eyes darted around in their fear.

What is a party if you cannot clink?

March, 2020

Green shoots poke through brown crusts of leaves,
encouraged by the early Spring;
two small robins prance across sodden grass.

The air is crisp yet warm.
The sun is high and invades your clothing,
you feel your chill effervescence.
Suspect Spring will bring to New England
the promise of flowers, the risk of late snow,
the defeat of Winter,
the suspicion of beaches and sweat,
the aroma of chowders and lobster rolls,
the cramp from ice cream gobbled too quickly,
tan days burning the reddish noses of Irishmen,
tee-shirts bulging with muscles,
tee-shirts stretched with bellies carrying memory of beers,
tee-shirts stretched over women's chests.

I envy Spring
with its laden promises,
its victory over cold,
its obliviousness to fear of failure,
its seasonal warmth,
its free ticket to the party
(and there are so few of those on offer in this world).

I am walking alone
because unlike Spring, people carry fear.
I cross the street when someone approaches,
I do not inhale when someone passes.

I do not smile
nor do I extend my hand for passing dogs to sample.

This is not a Spring of dreams.
Those Springs feel as an abstraction,
a ghost of other Springs,
a taunt, a dare.
This Spring will be remembered, no doubt,
as the non-Spring, the stifled Spring,
the Spring of poverty and death,
the Spring of babies conceived into unknown darkness.

I hope to live to write a poem about next Spring.
I hope then to understand, to decipher, to process, to explain.
I hope to reveal the message given us
by unseen Gods,
random fate,
not that the source is of moment.
I hope to chronicle the past,
inform the future,
instill all with flowers,
fill beaches with children,
gorge Churches with beliefs,
sleep on sand with women yet unborn
and recount this Spring
when crocus greens rushed upwards, unaware,
though no persons bent to see them.

No News is Good News

It is April of 2020 and no news is good news.
Whatever we read in the online newspapers,
whatever we see in our magazines,
whatever we see on the media news
is bad news, poverty and death.
Folks smarter than I do not read or listen to the news.
For them no news is good news.
The details of things are swamped by the reality of things,
sufficient anecdotes have infiltrated already,
sufficient cautions and fears have filled our minds
to the extent our minds need filling.
I will visit virtual museums from now on.
I will read poetry and novels from now on.
I will listen to opera and rap from now on.
I will visit websites of interest to others to see
if I am able to become interested.
I will delve into horse racing
and dog shows
and the design of kayaks
and the meaning of love
and the meaning of meanings.
And I expect
when dust settles on graves of all who find no solace
I will be a different person
both more distant from and
more empathetic towards everyone else.
It is raining outside my window.
It is dark and cold and wind-blown
and full of news outside my window.
No news is good news.

My Sequential Recordation of My Thoughts Upon Arising Today, April 10, 2020 at 8:14 AM In Newton Massachusetts

Contingent
    De/constructed
Di vided
Isolated
    aloft afloat flotsam
Dis/associated
    disaffected
    dis—what
    dissed
    done/undone
Unintegrated
Unremark/ed/able
Masked
Screened/linked
    alone with / out others
Stressing surpressing
Disfunctional working functioning
Prone to sardonic depression and to ascribe blame
Short of temper, devoid of empathy, out in a car low on gasoline looking for a gun store, an essential business in an existential time.

I was told
    how to act
        what was allowed
        who could come
            who must go

Let's not shake on it
You take my breath away
[I cannot see you]
      Gonna wash that XXXXX right outa my grasp
What words to say
Sucking wind in my mind
Pain
Imagined
      imaged
Now
No…….

As in now no what????
Tomorrow?

Where the hell are my slippers?

Love in the Age of Spring

Numbers, charts, slopes and graphs,
hospitals, mortuaries under-staffed.
Peaks, plateaus, flattened curves,
wearing masks, betrayed by nerves.
Dying in the old age home,
dying in cells, dying alone.
Crying about it does no good,
no salvation doing what you should.
Tempting to not have a care,
walk into crowds and take the dare.
Hopelessness, the enemy within,
calls out to commit social sin.
If I tried to kiss your lips today
would you run the other way,
or join me in the transient thrill:
is this kiss love, or will it kill?

And if I die before I close,
will you recall me with a rose?

Moment of Fame

He was a television star but did not care.
That was his hallmark, not caring.
He was virile if not viral, stripped to the waist in early Spring,
lean and pale and heading for the beach,
Spring Break on his mind,
and they stuck a camera in his face and asked him,
was he not afraid?
He was not.
He was not to be denied
what he thought his iconic entitlement,
of the beaches of Florida,
a mythic rite due to him, for what is his life worth
if not to live the life promised him.
And I first saw him on a newscast and thought him a fool.
Thereafter I saw him many times, in advertisements
and presentations of foolishness and danger,
of anti-social disregard,
of stupidity,
of assertion of the guilt he should feel
for causing such calamity to so many.
Is he alive today, I wonder.
I expect so or else the newsrooms would trumpet that
justice had been served.
Are those he loved alive today, and his roommates, and
even those casually in his path these last six weeks?

Do we wish him dead?
How would we feel if we learned it was true?
Do the careless die with our approval of their death,
the unthinking with a sense of our righteousness?

Do we, with a cheek still able to be turned,
bother to turn it
or do we curse his grave?
Who said that in a world of an eye for an eye
and a tooth for a tooth
we would all be gumming our gruel in darkness?

And if he survived, and continues now to survive
as we cautious citizens sometimes believe,
that the careless and condemned enjoy a cryptic special grace
not afforded to the upright folk who follow the rules,
will we just say "I knew it" with sad downward glance,
thinking of our friends who washed their hands and died with
clean finger-nails?

Do we hope that, if he lives,
he will learn from the error of his ways,
a thought so kindly to ourselves that it excuses our personal
confusion?
And if I hope he lives, and his older parents kissed him on his
return
and consoled him, and then died of that kiss,
if we see their boxes lowered into the ground
with only a few masked figures in attendance
and in the camera of our minds then see his face
and it is as stone
then do we wonder is he as shocked by his transgression
or thinking of the girls on the beach, and the life insurance.

I have thought of this young man often,
my mind first burying him in his polluted ground and then
resurrecting him in the grace of the God of men,
embarrassed that I should have been so hasty and unkind.

The debate goes on in my head
as I await my own fate
and a future newscast to answer my question.

Me and Katya in the Forest

I was sitting in my forest
as gently chill rain filtered through the branches
matting my hair.

My feet were cold, and it occurred to me
perhaps I might have worn shoes, but
too late, it is always too late.

Katya drifted in from the steppes
complaining the permafrost was melting
and history was oozing to the surface.

White light hung on drops effervescing
but failed to light our way.
Unicorns held back, shy as they are.

Pine scents dropped with wet needles
onto prickly ground,
some piercing between my toes.

Was it morning or was it Sabbath?
And whose, someone asked, not I nor Katya,
eyes averted lest caught gazing on the Deity.

Will She ascend today
to regain Her essence,
drawing Her tears back to clouds?

Will She descend today
to evaporate Her essence,
steam upon His fires?

Falcon dives killing sparrow
as coyote pounce killing fowl
and hunters kill to feather hats.
Bereft of birds. insects now rule.
Katya screams, eaten by wasps and worms.
I exult, kindred hearts abroad in my woods.

Tonight pine and oak will battle
and survive only as leaves and cones.
My forest culls itself each night as does the dying world.

Notebook Entries/June 2020

I drove a Lincoln into tomorrow.
All that power
and the inside smelled like leather.

Flowers bloom in tritely described gay profusion
but no one was laughing.
Perhaps there are hidden meanings…

Night proved unsettling as I settled into
thinking about the day that passed
and the cat stretched out in the moonlight.

If you remove batteries from a clock
you must know that time keeps advancing.
There is no doubt a course about that at major universities.

Claire and I set up an old telescope
and looked at the craters on the moon,
circles and presumed shadows.

Why do roads always go somewhere?
I would think that reflects lack of imagination.
Such a waste of gravel and concrete.

No one really understands Socrates.
He is often quoted, read on occasion
but revered only as an idea, abstractly.

Claire and I argued last night
over a tube of toothpaste.
She said squeezing in the middle is a sign of aggression.

Tomorrow I will count the money in my wallet.
This evening it counted forty-four dollars.
I wonder what will be there in the morning.

Dogs are easily distracted so we bought a cat.
Cats never do anything so cannot be distracted by definition.
Conservation of energy run rampant.

I feed the cat from my plate.
I started doing that after tasting from its bowl.
I never would let a sentient being dine like that.

The telescope is mine.
The Lincoln is a gift from Claire's parents.
The cat is community property.

Sometimes I spend entire days caring for myself.
I trim my beard, file my nails
and scrape dead skin off my heels with a rasp.

Some days I just write down my thoughts.
Claire then always says I should get a job
but I already have one.

I read in the New Yorker about two young actors
renovating a ranch house in New Jersey.
I called the magazine and asked why they ran that article.

Stephen M. Honig

I think my marriage to Claire is a mistake.
We have no interests in common.
I stay here only until our cat goes away to college.

Now is the time to contemplate my apple.
I do not eat apples.
I wish I had an apple, now.

There is dissonance in the universe,
particles we only imagine,
things scientists presume based on movements they do not understand.

When Claire slept with Harry I was not angry.
Harry is SO ugly!
So it did not matter.

Cats must understand dissonance
and all about roads.
That must be why they have given up on things.

Claire and I are leaving now for the movies.
She will trim her toe-nails first
so that she will look attractive in her sandals in the dark theater.

Fear (summer of 2020)

Whose fear do you carry when you're feeling so afraid?
Whom do you channel when you're sweating in your sheets?
Whom do you hate when you know you're being played?
Who is that behind you when you walk the midnight streets?

Are you worried for the babies in the ghettos without food?
Are you anxious for your children when they walk out your front door?
Do you think that death is stalking just because he's in the mood?
Do you jump a mile whenever there's a shadow on the floor?

There is warfare still lingering around half this rotting earth.
And poverty malingering in alley-ways and halls.
There are snitches who are fingering the strings of pain and dearth,
their echoes sound like bulges when the final judgment calls.

Do you fear they'll torch your house or vandalize your store?
Do you fear you'll breath too deeply and therefore breath your last?
Do you think they'll rape your daughter, calling her a whore?
Do you think that they'll uncover sins committed in your past?

This is the year of final sums, the ultimate accounting.
This is the moment petulant that kills and gives no reason.
Your fears are fears of everyone, each day you feel them mounting
'til you slip and slide to the underside to die in this dark season.

I welcome you to this cruel year when, locked within your room,
you look out through your window and contemplate your doom.
Then put you down this brittle page and curse your barren womb,
embracing entrance through wide doors to history's moist tomb.

August 1, 2020

It is a season of bad news
      from Washington to China,
      from Portland to Florida,
      from the whole earth.
Bad news we cannot cure,
useless to rail against.

Add to the list nature's bad news of the season:
today there are crabapples on the ground,
another event against which we are helpless.

And so, let us be depressed also by the crabapples.

Here is the story of crabapples because
I sense in you
confusion.

Crabapples are harbingers of Fall,
of clichéd chill winds,
of falling leaves carrying with them to the ground fragments of
my spirit.
Crabapples are canaries in the cage
set out by gods, grand designs or sciences
(it matters not)
to remind us
as we bask in sun
that Summer is on loan to us,

a best-seller to be sure, but therefore
with shortened rental period. reshelved upon
>	school bells
>	World Series
>	first frost,
Available next year for circulation
(if we are lucky).

And this year
a reminder of end of Summer
is not the melancholy sadness tempered by
cider, pumpkins, colored hills.
This year, melancholy sadness promises
children and families locked indoors,
no snowshoe and ski tracks,
no snowmen happily melting in sacrifice as we wait for the
carrot to fall.

They are early too, this year.
Did you not notice?
You might think a warmer world
would keep the glue on the stem longer,
the green-yellow fruit cemented in place.
But this is not just any year.
Old rules do not apply
when gods or grand designs or sciences
remind us while awake
what philosophers foster and clergy carp

and all of us learn some hour after midnight
suddenly upright in bed
    heart-felt beating
        eyes popped open as if there is something to be seen
        hints of sweat where sweat resides in wait,
when we say to ourselves
out loud
    "oh no
    more proof of my smallness
    my randomness
    my fear
    my death."

I have seen you on your walks these days.
You avert your eyes
    from other people,
    from dogs leashed and unleashed,
    from dirt, from trash, from crime,
    from offense and vulnerability.
Your isolation transmutes into aversion.
Therefore please add to your list:

Ignore the crabapples.

They are up to no good.

Take it from a man who knows.

Suburban Halloween Party

Party on my deck.
Masks required.
Not what you're thinking—
Halloween.

Mother Teresa just slipped out of the kitchen.
She's got her eye on some poor guy....

It's been weird this past summer.
We all stopped counting
> the ill
> the dead
> the unemployed
> the riots
> the stock market.

At least liquor stores stayed open.

Jaded.
Yes we are.
Yes indeed.
A trio in the corner plays Vivaldi
and Carmina Burana without the words.
We stand close, but are happy for the masks
now that they are not a political statement.

We are drinking my fine French reds.
Be damned if I'll die with the 2000s and 2010s undrunk!
The young people, angry there's no beer or spiked seltzer
are dropping club soda and maraschinos into $150 cabernets.

Well, doesn't matter, they'll likely survive—
Live and learn.

POTUS has cloned;
orange hair abounds.
Red ties over black T-shirts.
The best one has a huge phallus over his shoulder.
So sad.

Harry came carrying a small coffin.
The cover said "America has gone to pot."
Inside, just a lot of marijuana.
Legalized grass killed the suburban coke market
(or maybe it's the economy).

I have assiduously invited every black person I know.
Neither of them came.

Couples are sick of each other.
No one is talking to their spouse.
Nor are they divided by sexes.
They are re-paired,
seeking a flirt which they know will not survive the night.

I look at the pile of paper plates, plastic utensils and glasses,
all going to trash.
In my closet, five bags of wipes.
Cleopatra and Napoleon and Elvis may die
but not in my house, if I can help it.

Did I mention my mother died in June?
She got sick without leaving her house.
The sardonic say, "when your time comes, you're gone."

Stephen M. Honig

That assumes there is a God who assigns you your hours.
Ain't no God in a pandemic,
only people who think otherwise.

In the corner, Madonna is bragging
she shorted the market just before the September crash.
The centaur she is talking to is silent, fidgety.
That's Lou from next door
and I bet he went long before the ax fell.

It's one AM and no one will leave.
That's because there is no tomorrow,
only another yesterday.
At least I am drunk.
When I end up in bed,
I can just pass out and won't have to make any excuses.

Thanksgiving Tent

The Israelite sat in a tent,
hoping the desert wind would not blow it away.
Looking up at the million burning stars,
he wondered who he was and why he was alive,
if the Sea next day would swallow him up,
and was that the distant plod of horses coming closer across the night?
He thanked his God in fear of not doing so
and in fear he had been misled about the future.

The knight stood in his tent beneath the peak
as his groom unclasped his breast shield,
struggling to keep it from falling to the rug below.
He wondered if the battle next day
would give him mortal wounds so that he would die
alone below the million burning stars.
He begged his God to stand by him, certain He would but
in the corner of his resolve lurked mortal fear.

The Pueblo sat in his kiva watching the smoke rise through the roof
to obliterate the sight of the million burning stars
as he drank the fermented cactus juice in near-catatonic dreams
and fretted of the scout's report of army regulars across the gulch
in numbers too large to scorn.
He implored Earth his mother to protect him in her womb,
glanced furtively at the sipapu portal to the darkness,
but did not sleep lest he failed to hear the long guns at first dawn light.

The man sat beneath a sagging tent
staring at turkey bones and a dish of orange potatoes.
Rain traveled gently along the seams, dripping occasionally
onto dirty dishes sitting on the folding card table.
Above, the million burning stars vainly glowed,
denied entry by clouds of two descriptions.
Silently, he thanked the powers that brought him through this day
and then prayed vaguely for tomorrow.

Holiday Poem

It is Christmas
and the world bleeds down the face of time.
The day's news is full of pain and sorrow,
people die by gun, by disease, by accident,
by war, by starvation.

It is Channukah
and the world bleeds down the face of time.
The day's news is full of pain and sorrow.
People die by hate, by prejudice, by indifference,
by genocide, by tribal lust.

It is yesterday, it is tomorrow,
and the world bleeds down the face of time.
Its red drops soak into Bibles, into Torahs,
into Upanishads, into Kojikis,
into the Seven Valleys and the Four Valleys.

It is the Holidays and all rejoice for what they have.
Or what they want.
Or what they have stolen
or killed
or dominated.

And there is a fire
of blood-stained holy books
position papers and treaties
lamentations and apologia
which burns into the night and does not die.

The blood of people who believe
pools at the foot of mountains.
The sea may have parted, but
blood does not part by whim of deities.
We are drowning, we are drowning....

Colored Lights

(Written with our lights still hanging after a passing thunderstorm. This poem is a memory of the future).

We have strung small colored lights across our porch
to welcome our few visitors in this curious time
where masks cover smiles
which we must imagine.
We are destined to be home for many months.
We have seen our lights strive against the storms of March,
dance in the rains of April,
float among the wisps of May,
dodge the pollens of June,
bask in Summer heat,
undulate on Fall winds and, we presume,
shiver by battering Winter until,
one night in December,
our lights frosted over with icy glaze so heavy,
down they will fall, hooks pulled from shingles,
dropped in near-silent tinkles
by the weight of the world.

Next morning we may try to pick up the shards of glass
glowing red and yellow and green,
sticking up pertly through a sheen of icy snow
but find the glass fused coldly to the ground,
Not moveable without unexpected cuts
and hardly worth the effort,
to sort out that which was frigid from that which was sharp.

And so it stayed, all of it.

The dog did not understand why he could not exit the porch door
as was his style.
The concept of denial does not resonate with dogs.
Through January frosted and snowy
and February bitter and blown with dry purpose,
through snows wet and heavy, frothy and light,
glass sometimes glistening in stolid air
and sometimes hiding in random drifts,
until one day in March,
perhaps the anniversary of the lights,
the shards fall free in the melt,
to be swept up and poured into a random tin pail,
colored memories of hard times resisted by light,
conversations with friends who will return
to share our porch
(well, a few will not)
with neither masks nor illusions.

We will not be inclined to string new lights that Spring.
They were a consolation and a promise
but also a witness to memories.
It is better sometimes to sit in darkness than to create false light.

If some years from now
you were to go down our cellar stairs,
turn right into the earthy room
that houses a water heater and unused oil tank,
stored garden tools,
boxes of books for which there is no more room and thus
sit in growing mold,
then turn back under the stair and look in that wooden crate
with brownish slats and no cover

you will see a pail full of colored glass fragments.
You will wonder why, but I suspect you will understand.
Some things need to be remembered but not dwelt upon.
Voices echo in the pail,
captured in time and space we call memory.
I will not discard the pail and I will not look inside it.
The pail will mean so much to me—
but I cannot yet say what that is.

Disorder

I cannot understand who I am.
This is likely a common problem among people
but I am much more interested in my confusion than in yours.

I live in a house where I am the oldest person.
I have become uncomfortable with cold.
My son goes to school in the snow wearing shorts and sandals.
It is not to spite me, it is after all his affair
and his feet.
But this disorder in my house means others turn down the heat
while I sneak to the controls and turn up the heat.
People are angry with me and blame me
for their respiratory ills.
My finger-tips ache.
I wear gloves and warming inserts.
Our only common grounds is the fireplace
where radiant warmth is accepted by all,
for some a romantic scene,
for me a respite.

I cannot read the newspapers.
I am not alone in this world I am sure.
I am not surprised that newspapers are in decline.
Who can stand the harping presence of ill tidings
sitting on your lap, present without your choosing,
demanding implicitly your mind's eye,
feeding your personal disorder?

I am neat but not overly clean.
I am of the out-of-sight-out-of-mind school

where disorder is fought by neatness.
At home, physical disorder is kept spotlessly clean but
left in full display.

I have a list of things I must do today.
It is Saturday morning, and today I start
living my life by doing the important things
that cannot be reached during the work week.
I am this morning sitting here writing this poem
which is not on my list.
You do not write on your list in the evening:
>   work on taxes
>   shop for underwear
>   read last Sunday's Times magazine
>   write a long poem
>   dry the laundry.

Today is a sad day.
A son of friends passed away last week.
Disorder's middle name is Death,
a visitor of chaos excused for rudeness when old people die
but is hated when Death visits the young.
If your life seems down-hill over time
and you judge the lives of others similarly,
why do you assume the young who die are losing a life
ascendant?
Perhaps because life itself is ascendant
and all we have to boot?
It is all part of disorder, and today
I will stand in a graveyard
in chill wind
feel tears dry on my crinkled cheeks
avoid looking at other people

and tonight join a celebration of a lost life
of the boy who made everyone smile
who hugged adults on meeting them,
ultimate sweetness not to be derided here
midst this poem of disorder and despair.
We will smile at each other's memories
and tell ourselves it is acceptable
as we have no choice.

You do not know this boy
so you must trust me
that his passing
leaves in the air the trace of Evangeline's music.

Four people died yesterday of a strange virus.
They lived across the country.
I read this part of the newspaper
as four deaths of people I do not know
can be tolerated, I suppose.
They are all of them of my generation.
It seems that Death is coming in disguise,
to evade denial.
I must put my affairs in order,
starting today, as
one never knows,
does one?

Real Reel

Goin' to the movies every day these days.
Closed up, but I got a couple of 'em I know how to get in,
jimmy the side doors, no one cares.
They are hot or they are cold but I don't mind.
I love the movies and every night they play my favorites.
I used to sit close, first row, so the thing filled my eyes and mind
and no one in front to distract me,
but now I sit in the balcony, line up my candy next to me
and watch the old ones
when comedy was, you know, funny
and made no bow to the dark side of the world.
My favorite is Groundhog Day because the asshole wins the girl
because he isn't an asshole any more
which is sort of uplifting, right?
And Airplane. And the Marx brothers—
God damn, I love the Marx brothers.
Not Chaplin. His world is dark and
I'm here inside, Fall of 2020, watching the big screen
and laughing my butt off.
And it's good because it's free
and they are always playing my favorite of the day
--how do they know, huh?—
and if I gotta pee they just stop the movie right there
and when I come back they start right back up
and don't miss a beat.
One time I asked my friend Louis to join me and
we sneaked in, sat down and I started the movie
and after a few minutes he said I was nuts and I said,
why Louie, don't you like Abbott and Costello
and then he looked at me hard for a minute

which I could feel in the dark though my flashlight was out
--don't use a flashlight unless you are the usher—
and next I knew I heard the side door slam,
metal shaking in the jamb.

A Walk On the Wild Side

Took a walk in the park,
careful to keep my distance.
Pleased to see, like me,
just about everyone was wearing a mask.

There was:
Barbie, dressed as Barbie the Nurse.
Iron Man, and Lone Ranger, naturals.
A man with a mask in front and in back, whom I assume to be two-faced.
A person carrying a sign with a picture on a pole of his quarantined mother.
A person carrying a sign with a black-draped picture of his late father
and a man with no mask, but a red cap and a sign saying
> "if you don't like it, too bad because my nickname is Hidden Cary."

Then there was the mask walking down the path to the pond with no person
> which proves even the invisible man is compliant.

I walk a lot these days.
You meet the most interesting people.

About the Sky in Time of Pandemic

Outside my window this morning
there is a sense of diffused light,
leaking through white cloud-puffs,
drifting around patches of blue sky.

The day cannot make up its mind.
I am awaiting its verdict.
I can sink into my chair with indifference,
abjuring the taking of the air, or
declare it will rain, as by personal fiat, or
plan a sojourn and attend to it
regardless of weather and consequence.

Or, I can close my drapes.
The sky then can do its will.
If it is something I do not know, then
it will not happen.

Ambivalence is the new normal.

Dead Men Walking....

dead men, women, kids young old who knows
sick shot parlayed and played
traded down rivers for small change
masked and still naked and still counting
lots of totals lots of graphs
dead everybodies walking around my mind
dragging at me, pulling at me
don't like it
at all
but
no one asked me
here in the Fall of America
here watching the fall of America.

writing this while I still can 10-7-20
anyone out there to read it?

Gray

It is moving towards night and low to the hazed horizon
there is a slate gray cloud from one end of my vision to another.
And at its puffy top, gray clouds going to black, speaking to me of rain
wind
chill.
A sea gull flutters, rare
as they usually glide; there is wind in currents out there.
He or she is gray with dapples and flashes of white and black,
a complexity of no color.
The gull rests on the railing outside my window and stares at me.
There is the gray of no understanding in its stare.
My windowpane should be clear but it too is gray,
the outside monotone seems to coat the surface of the glass,
I have painted glass
as if I am not looking through it but at it, it has its own pretensions to colors
and it sports gray bubbles of rain that reflect the gray which is so gray.
The city is below; its buildings gray by color and spirit and design
sitting on gray streets while, between two buildings,
the harbor is a flat gray plain, its ripples too far away to break the tone.

There is an infinite continuum of grays, starting at some subtle place
just East of white and marching away towards the black horizon
to the undividing line of the West rim of black.
There is no difference among the white and black and their

proxies, serfs, minions, pretenders, hopers....
How do you tell the men in the white hats from the others?
Seems you need not bother, everyone is some variant of gray,
you are by definition wasting your time,
fiddling with fractions,
messing with millimeters,
classifying clouds that change even as you say
this one is an X, and that one over there definitely a Y
and there are not enough letters.

It is all melting back into itself,
without verve or personality, the whole visible world in retreat
back to its own dark beginnings.
The start of the world perhaps is red as red is life,
But the end place is black.

Aspects of gray are stepping-stones to ebony and then
all of it is gone home to die.

It's the End

It's the end, alright.
Oh, it's the end.
You may not believe it but
we don't run on your beliefs.

It's the end of the day,
darking flowing into dark,
the angry hours,
but that's not the end that cuts.

It's the end of love,
hating flowing into hatred,
the agony hours,
but that's not the end that cuts.

It's the end of earth,
rotting flowing into rotten,
the crying hours,
but that's not the end that cuts.

It's the end of me,
flesh flowing into earth,
the dying hours,
but that's not the end that cuts.

It's the end of everything.
It's the end of light and love and lust and earth and wind and sky
and fire and flesh and fine strands of truth curling up from the
smoldering people
and warmth turning away the chill of nothingness and forever.

When this poem reaches its end you will feel a jarring shake to your universe and that will be the last thing you will ever know--but you won't know that, will you, because it is the absolute end.

Stephen M. Honig lives in Newton, Massachusetts with his wife, the youngest of his four children, and one recalcitrant dog. As of this writing, everyone in his household wears masks except for the cock-a-poo. This is Steve's third book of poetry, following a collection entitled *Messing Around With Words* and a chapbook entitled *Rail Head*. He notes that, finally, he has encountered a reality exceeding his long-held dark view of the universe; he has attempted in this work to capture the human edge of that reality. He knowingly joins the inevitable flow of poetry in that attempt. "The aggregate of that flow will constitute the true history of our time."

www.ingramcontent.com/pod-product-compliance
Lightning Source LLC
LaVergne TN
LVHW011859060526
838200LV00054B/4423